The Beast and The Innocent

Diana Pinckney

FUTURECYCLE PRESS
www.futurecycle.org

Library of Congress Control Number: 2015932560

Copyright © 2015 Diana Pinckney
All Rights Reserved

Published by FutureCycle Press
Lexington, Kentucky, USA

ISBN 978-1-938853-71-5

for Francis, for family, for friends

Contents

I

An Artist Speaks to Her Unborn Paintings..................9
The Dance..................10
La Maddalena..................11
Ghost Wolves, for My Grandchildren..................12
Fallen Gardens..................13
American Tourist, Normandy..................14
Raised by Wolves..................15
The Coal Bin..................16
The Trapper Looks Back..................18
Gray Wolf to Dog..................19
Yeats Exhibit, Downstairs National Library, Dublin..................20
Soir Bleu, 1914..................21
A Senator Celebrates..................22
Little Red on YouTube..................24
She Had Some Dogs..................25
A Spinster Considers Her Options..................26
The Snake Handler's Wife Has Her Say..................28

II

Elizabeth Plays Alice..................31
The Bridge Game..................32
Rosabelle's House..................33
This..................34
Behind the Kitchen Door..................36
Straightening Pictures..................37
Storytime..................38
The Magic Bed..................39
The Kiss of Water..................40
After Andy,..................42
Between Worlds..................43
Red Wolf to Coyote..................44
The Man Who Loves Broken Things..................45
The Woman Who Loves Takeout..................46

Melancholia	47
Goddamnitalltohell	48
Music	49
Pawnee to Wolf	50
Letter to Sallie in Mallorca	52
Songlines	53
The Beast and The Innocent	54
My Brother Sings	55
Winged Wolf	56
After the Hands	57
Author's Note	59
Acknowledgments	

I

It is myself that I remake.

—W. B. Yeats

An Artist Speaks to Her Unborn Paintings

My hand holds no brush.
This dish is what I have. And children,
lovely clatter of voices flooding the days.
Eggs scrambled, boys off to school.
The little one plays dolls
while another sleeps, her weeks-old breath
rowing ceaseless, hungry

while I dream canvasses stretching
outlines on ocher-soaked linens,
earth-dug umber, sienna, yolk yellows,
wet, oily and waiting to bleed
thick and gummy from the brush,
the scent, an ether in my veins,
leaves me lightheaded, anointed
by the gods I might have stolen from.

Now the baby cries
and here she is, moist,
smelling of milky cotton, absorbing
this minute, the hazy hours. I'll spill years
to her as the earth changes faces,
greens of summer rusting into autumn
and, in winter, the north light
catching fire in the braids of her hair.

The Dance

after Botticelli's Annunciation, Uiffizi Gallery

The virgin turns her body from the news,
smooth palms fending off the Angel

of Annunciation. God's messenger
has dipped to one knee as in proposal.

Mary's shoulders slope
like folded wings, a bird poised to fly

through the open doorway
past a garden and the lone tree

splayed out against blue sky.
Gabriel holds a long reed, a quill

ready to write her story. Mary offers
her eggshell face, beautiful in the way

of all Botticelli's dazed Madonnas,
eyes downcast or gazing into a future

his fledgling angels,
those dreamy boys, are spared.

La Maddalena

after Donatello, Museo del Duomo

This statue, Magdalene out of
the desert, out of a poplar's gnarled stump

in a gallery of marble men,
a woman created from wood.

Matted hair a web of worms
preserved in polychrome,

Magdalene waits,
alone among stone-eyed saints.

In an agony of age, Donatello carved
this old Mary far from the grace

of forgiveness, her body and face honed
to bones, the way my mother looked

after surgery. In the bed
where her leg had been,

a hollow. Her eyes staring,
as if watching for something coming.

Ghost Wolves, for My Grandchildren

You may see one in a zoo
    and ask, does he howl
        and I may say, what would

he howl about? What, you ask, does a wild
    wolf sound like? What could I answer? Wind
        when it rises from the deepest

canyon to the tops of spruce
    or the fog's blue surge, the drift
        above dying embers. Smoke alone

moves toward the stars in a world
    where nothing is heard and only the moon
        knows when the last tree falls.

Emptiness that whispers
    after the wilderness
        has forgotten what it longs for.

Fallen Gardens

April leaves its glory to the warmth
and whims of May, another dry summer
in the forecast. Doesn't the end of any month
ache to return to beginnings—tender

green opening to white, white to green,
even though the stunning fullness
of a branch bent with pale blossoms
is never enough to bring back a son.

No breeze can gentle the knowledge
that somewhere in old Babylon
a father pleads for Allah, for any god
to grant him Abraham's deliverance.

Bereft of angels, his sky instead
carries a stinging wind circling the man
forced by soldiers to lower a gun
to the crown of his son's head,

a young informer broken
to the ground at his father's feet,
his forehead pressed in dust
that will rise and cover us all.

American Tourist, Normandy

No greener grass cradles this vast sea
    of crosses flowing north, south, east, each row
        facing west. Straight white paths,
            some markers topped with a six-pointed
                Star of David. Chiseled on marble,

name after name until you face a stone
    of the *Unknown*. Under clipped trees, clouds
        like parachutes, chimes muffling a battle hymn,
            you walk toward the *Wall of the Missing*
                where a guide, speaking French,

is leading a group. They pass, a man stops,
    looks right at you and quietly says, *Merci,*
        then in English, *Thank you so very much.*
            You, in your hat and sunglasses
                on this June day. You, who have not hung

like a puppet on the bell tower of *Sainte Mere Eglise,*
    have not been pinned to the hedgerow bluffs
        and tumbling walls of Omaha Beach,
            never jumped from those now decaying *Mulberries,*
                Sir Winston's floating harbors, into the ocean's churn

below this ground. You have not clawed up
    ninety-foot *Pointe Du Hoc* through all the dying
        of all you know. Safe and dry above the water,
            you stand looking down toward the cliffs
                of Utah Beach, home to a scatter of gulls

while somewhere on this hundred seventy-two acres,
    among the nine thousand three hundred
        eighty-seven stars and crosses,
            someone's baby cries, a sound that lingers
                then washes out to sea.

Raised by Wolves

after Jim Goldberg's installation at the San Francisco MOMA

Loaded tables like a yard sale. Step closer. A tangle
of Nikes and gloves without
fingers—no lefts or rights—ripped knapsacks, belts
with silver buckles unbuckled, knives,
mascara tubes, needles, sling pumps,
guns, sunglasses, empty
plastic bags, metal pieces glinting
under the skylight.

Walk along white walls
crowded with girls and boys in black
and white photos, smiling
up at you from mattresses. Piercings, tattoos
and bruises—*all that vulgar beauty*—
decorate punctured arms laced around
each other. The writing
under the pictures is cursive—squat,
round vowels, consonants
slanted—children scribbling on walls.

What is not written. How many
are out there? How hard
is it to go home after the street? What flickers

in the corner? A runaway's home video loop. Sit, watch pink
cheeked dolls, a red tricycle, balloons, a cake with three
trick candles—lighting, re-lighting, rosy
mouth barely over the tabletop, blows and blows.

The Coal Bin

after Elizabeth Bishop

The President died today, my friend
Lila tells me, her hand on her heart.
I am seven. It is 1945. A war is
going on. Each night in bed, I replay
my brother's story—*Germans
in our cellar, behind the coal bin*—I whisper
to Lila, who cries when I challenge her

to walk across the hall grate covering
the furnace that heats our house. She's
a little mouse with papery skin and hair,
with pale eyes that water when I describe
submarines under waves thrumming
toward her family's beach cottage, how
at the stroke of midnight, little men
will crawl through dunes to the porch, moonlit
hammocks creaking. Lila vows not to go

this summer or ever. Opening the cellar
door, my father starts down
to stoke the furnace. *Ridiculous,*
he answers when I ask about
the enemy below. *Stop your foolishness,*
Mother says, bending to the radio's
wooden arc that drums of battles, each
day's news attended to, each night's blackout
secured by shades dark as Father's slick black

coat and hat he wears out the door,
an air-raid warden on rounds. Tonight, after
he hangs his hat on its rusty porch hook,
after the house clanks and groans

into sleep, I dare myself downstairs
to the hallway. The furnace rumbles—
Step on me—commands—*do it*—
one leap over the hot grate—
I'm on the other side.
It is 2012. War is going on.

The Trapper Looks Back

after Barry Lopez's Of Wolves and Men

Trapping's different. Takes time and knowing. What a wolf
knows, what he likes. Fix your blind set, just below the dirt
with rotten meat right by. Or there's your scent set,
dusted with some varmint's tail. You wait. Wait some more.
Might hear a kinda scream, then a crazed, high

wailing. Some days you follow where that ole boy dragged
the trap. Could be miles trailing blood. A wolf don't go down
till each danged leg gives way. Pelts bring more than wolf
ears or dead pups turned in for bounty. Solids—
white, black, them stone blues
from up north—put extra change in your pocket,

depending on who's buying. It ain't like
I never had a dog. Wolves is different. Vermin, cowpokes
calls 'em. We all had our ways to kill
the wolf—ranchers hired guns, hunters put out strychnine,
government paid by the kill. Some done worse—track down
a den, reach in, pull out the pups. Little fellas...think you want

to play. They make low yips, whines, rubbing up
to you. Catch 'em by the throat. Been told they go limp
quick in a man's grip. Still, it can take a man
off to the bushes, sick as any dog.
Wild animals is smart. Wolves more so. I switched my traps

from smooth to toothed. Got a 60-foot chain. Nowadays, sitting
in my trailer, I think on what wildness is out there. Seems like
the land's gone lonely. Can't help but look
for them big four-toed prints. Once an old white
whined, looked straight at me, his trapped foot held out.
I was flat broke. That one stays with me.

Gray Wolf to Dog

I passed you, cousin, chained
by your dry bowl, when I trotted my starved
body to the edge of town. Down
on the banks of the river, nothing leapt
from shallow rocks,
no fat heads with soft eyes, not one

flapping silver tail to move mine. Nothing
but light and shale shimmering
in September's heat. Not one cloud
pulled the red fish here. Not one drop
for the creek bed. No salmon
and only berries for the bear. You, dog,
never rolled in the dark

snows of tundra, never knew
the secrets of cedars. You, who whined
for scraps and dodged their sticks,
are free. And when they come home
with the crimson sun,
their pockets and pails empty,

they will find strings of fur, curls
of white tinged with pink at the end
of a chain. Because of you, I live
another day to follow the wood's
scented trails, to run
under the shadow of the owl.

Yeats Exhibit, Downstairs National Library, Dublin

Walls ripple with birds, a screen
      of words, the lake of lines mirror swans. On a bench
          a young man moves his lips to the music

of words, a voice reading "The Wild Swans
      at Coole." The man's coat, his wavy black hair
          and profile, classic Yeats. He owns this space

I dare not enter. The swans at Coole, the reflections
      of water his alone. No windows, no sun
          light Yeats's world. A hall of photographs winds

to Maude, to Georgie, young and bright on the wall.
      Isolde shimmers. Here's Ben Bulben, there's the tower,
          home to no one, not lover,

not wife. Letter boxes, poems with lines crossed
      through. Blots of brown on pages covering
          desks. Inkpots, Ouija boards, tarot cards.

From the room of scrolled poems, a voice
      calls me back to the bench, now empty,
          my young Yeats flown with the swans.

Rolling lines of "Easter, 1916" cover rubble, men who fall and jerk
      across a screen of bloodied horses. Next
          the shelled Post Office, rebels lined up.

One holds a flag, flapping like a white bird. I'm left with
      a drumroll of names. Who can know
          the present from the past?

Soir Bleu, 1914

after Edward Hopper

I want to table-hop, join the elegant
couple wearing gold and a tux, to sip from blue
goblets, move to the turtle-necked man, black
beret, sexy mustache. These drinkers flank the star
of this terrible cafe, the clown—bald head

a moonscape, red mouth drooping
a cigarette—whose costume bleeds
white onto the table where he deals seven-
card stud while the madam
in low-cut purple stands behind him as if they

are partners, arms and swelling breasts her claim
to white, a Cassandra who carries a prophesy
and knows that the gentleman with Navy epaulettes
on his shoulders will wash the deck
with blood just as the clown, color

of death, foresees these others swallowed
by swollen trenches, a carnage that failed to end
all wars. Even Hopper in prewar
Paris couldn't fathom
the numbers that would rot

in those ditches and bloated fields, so many that old
Monet, driven to larger and larger
works as each day brought stories
from the front, name upon name, could never
cover his canvas with enough water lilies.

A Senator Celebrates

> *The 71st U.S. Congress legislated not less than 10 million dollars to control predatory animals, a bill signed into law by President Hoover, March 31, 1931.*

How good it is to be in the heart
of this God-given, God-graced
land. Here on July 4th with people who
have the grit to conquer what threatens.
You who broke your backs farming, raising

those flocks and herds. Remember
the slick calf you pulled from a moaning,
bellowing cow? Is that little calf safe?
Are your sheep and, yes, even
your little children, Lord bless 'em,

safe from the killer at the gate? Yes, friends,
I speak of the wolf. Dog of the Devil,
shadow that lurks at the edges of forests
and fields, the doors of barns, a night raider
circling your fences, the very homes

you built. Now Congress has given us
the means to use whatever it takes—
guns, traps, cyanide, strychnine pellets—
to rid the earth of a dangerous predator. University
types have protested the extermination

of this scourge, predicting the wolf's
decline. I say do not listen. Science
says the wolf will always find a way
to breed. Do-gooders. Who among them
has ever seen a hungry farm child,

seen a half-eaten, bloodied lamb? I say
the Devil take them and his beast with them.
They are not us. They have no concern
for my record, your voice in Washington. You know
I'm a conservationist, saving wildlife

for our parks, our hunting grounds. Come,
my friends, let's celebrate this new bill.
Wave your red, white and blue, boys
and girls, for the wilderness
tamed and farmed for you.

Bow your heads in the cottonwoods'
shade and bless the labors of your hand
and mine. Give thanks for those tables
laden with barbecue, chops and ribs, gifts
from the good Lord and our good land.

Little Red on YouTube

True story from a girl with curls in a red hoodie. Here's what went down that day I met Big Bad hanging on the path, humming growl-like. Gave me the shivers. Great hair, too. And, OMG, that killer grin. He asked where I was headed and *Could I carry your basket, lovey?* No problem. That sherry was a load. I hand it over, point the way and he whistles himself along. What a wicked walk. I tooled around with flowers, butterflies. Screwed up big time when I yakked about Wolfie to Mr. Huntsman who wondered if I had seen a tall, dark stranger. Time I got to my grandma's—Hello! Big Bad's under the covers with Granny, laughing, cutting up. Man. Her lace cap's off, empty bottle under the nightstand, cake crumbs all over. Hot-shot Huntsman barges in. Whacks Wolfie. My sweet granny died on the spot. Shock? Shame? Who says an old lady's not allowed to party? A dude swinging an axe, that's who. Huntsman's now sheriff, mega-hero on Facebook, TV—you name it. What's with this kill stuff? That's just, you know, mean. And the lies forever after.

She Had Some Dogs

who loved her too much.
She had some dogs
who followed her all her life. She had
a beauty they couldn't resist, a voice
so warm and deep, they folded
at her feet. She had some dogs
big and small, black and white, red,
white and brown. She named one Flush
after Elizabeth Barrett Browning's dog.
She watched as he followed her little girl
running across the street. Red clay, red
blood, red and white fur is what the girl
will always see. Prince died
under the card table as she played her kings
and queens. Sonny, of the fierce love,
saved a night watchman's life
after she gave him to the man. She had
some cats, but that's another
story. The girl who ran had some dogs
and her own story. But her mother had
bad legs and, at the end, only the crazy dog
who chewed the rug madly as she
lay in her bed, wanting to die.

A Spinster Considers Her Options

For a long time now I have tried to think
of a nice way to kill Papa. He's stubborn
as God and just as remote. Other old men
die. He's lived on, hunched over his Latin
and Greek. Pulled those study doors together
while Mama scraped to get us by, so thin
when she died you could read a newspaper
through her hand.

I take in boarders now, put food on a table
crowded with men lonelier
than I am. They're afraid
of Papa. He stares down any fellow
who dares to speak
or hold a door for me.

I've no stomach to poison the tea—
just want him gone, God forgive me, clean gone.
Cousin Albert, his favored nephew till that day
Papa stumbled on us in the garden.
Only a baby bird we bent to watch.
Albert took the evening train
back to Lynchburg. For a time
I heard from him by post.
But, really, that was all so long ago.

Not near enough automobiles to hope
for an accident on Papa's walk.
Though, regular as rain, Mr. Thornben's Packard
hops the curb, driving being so strange
and all. Fire's too risky. Papa would get out
and my box of letters from Albert burn instead.

Dusting in the study this morning
while Papa read, I noticed his oak bookcase
had begun to tilt of late. And late
it is. The boarders will soon arrive
for midday dinner. I must snap some beans
before I have to stop and run to see
what on earth has made that awful crash.
Then I'll call our Dr. Penefield. Surely
Cousin Albert will come for Papa's service.

The Snake Handler's Wife Has Her Say

You Wildlife folks got it wrong. No way God's creatures don't love Jake. The man don't have a mean bone in that blessed body. Neither do them snakes. 'Course I got the jitters when my babies started crawling around the house. Sometimes Jake forgot to lock every cage out back and one'd creep in and curl round a bed leg or under the sink. Yeah, they's looking for heat and water. Then, 'cause the State said so, we moved 'em to the Tabernacle. Still our young'uns growed up fine, one boy crazy to this day 'bout them animals. No matter what the law says, God wants us worshippin' the way the Bible teaches. I swear, you oughta see Jake at church with snakes hanging 'round his neck—two at a time and another looking ready to purr, wrapping Jake's legs, swaying up, trying to reach those gentle hands. He strokes, then moves dance-like, twisting his head and hips. Lordy, you'd think Elvis done come back. Jake gets agoing and I gets agoing. Excited. Right there in church. Jesus help me. Them some kinda hands. One night, me and Jake was weaving together so sweet we slid right off the bed. He's maybe thinking I'm more snake than Eve. I'm just thinking—Jake. Praise the Lord. The State oughta leave us be—the church, Jake, Jake Jr., and the faithful—all grateful to God and snake holding. Next time your men barge in, strutting down the aisle, that fat old Sheriff, bless his heart, trailing behind, you better watch it. No tellin' who's gonna get bit.

II

I know who I was when I got up this morning, but I think I must have been changed several times since then.

—Lewis Carroll, *Alice's Adventures in Wonderland*

Elizabeth Plays Alice

Crossing a park at age eight,
hair long and blonde, my mother
heard a voice, *You're Alice, my Alice.*

I'm Elizabeth, she told the man.
But he directed the town theatre
and she played in Wonderland.

Once an actor forgot his cue, little Alice
boomed the last line, called them all
a pack of cards, brought down the house.

When her mother took in boarders,
Alice resented strange hats in the hall,
the changing cups and faces at the table.

With callers by the dozen, she chose
my father who gave her a garden with thorns.
Alice was the Queen of Hearts in a full

house where her mother stayed the longest,
leaving finally at ninety-four.
Alone then, unable to stop the darkness

that climbed from the bad foot,
Alice said, *Of all those gone,
I miss Mama most.* At her bedside no words,

no magic, could keep her from growing
smaller in that room where the light stayed on
all night and she was gone by morning.

The Bridge Game

I find my father
in what they call the Rec Room
on the eighth floor, doors locked,
nurses carrying keys

in starched white pockets. He brightens
when he sees me and rises
from the chair, handing me
his cards. *My daughter will take my place,*

thank you. He nods to the other three
at the table, winks at me. Away he slips
to the plateglass window we'd stood by
the night before, both of us looking down

on the blinking cars and lights of a street
he puzzled over. Was this the city where
he had lived for forty years or a street
in the small town of his youth, he'd asked.

I know it as the street where he
was found two days ago in his bathrobe,
hailing a cab. Now I listen
as my fellow players

bid up and down, over the top—
nonsensical, diamonds and spades
interchangeable. Like Alice,
at croquet with the Queen of Hearts,

I have to play his hand in a game of Jokers
Wild, all the rules changed.

Rosabelle's House

I'd learned the way by holding
her hand for the few blocks that separated
our houses, after a while arriving
on my own at Rosa's front stoop to ask
for Maybelle, her youngest. The two of us
lured doodlebugs up sticks stirred
in loose dirt, chanting, *Your house is
on fire, your children do roam.* Or we smashed

and picked oily nuts dropped by the tree
behind a house thick with hot air, fragrant
with the tobacco Rosa's ancient mother
chewed and fried chicken draining
on paper sacks. Through gaps
in the floorboards, dust mingled
the musty smells—every worn piece
of clothing and linen passed from our home

to hers—blankets, pillows, spreads
stacked in corners, shoved
under beds. Nothing refused. Radios
that could not speak. Lamps, toasters,
fans in those three rooms with no power.
Sometimes we sat on the back steps
under the pecan's merciful
green. From the doorway Little Mama,

shriveled into a chair's cave that spilled
cotton the color of her hair, gave rise
to a grainy voice, *A band of angels
coming for...*and Rosa answered
from the kitchen, *Swing low,*
while Maybelle and I bent over the peas
we were shelling, one bowl filling as the other
emptied, hands touching, then moving apart.

This

after The House That Jack Built

This is the mother of that
young man who did
those things to that girl
found in the sand
by the river under the bridge

did this mother dress the boy in navy
and white a boy with almost
all A's the teacher's praise his book
bag tidy his bike shiny

isn't this the woman who buried
the canary let out
of its cage by that
same boy who played

with strays the woman
who found the cat curled
and still under
the pillow under
the sill who didn't

spot the blood
under his nails turning
her head at what
the cop said

what
of the other
mother who ribboned
hair and buckled shoes
all polished and red of that
small girl who spilled

juice over the table
down her legs this
mother who scolded
that girl before
she played in front-yard

shade in sand that stuck
to her legs before
the car with that nice
young man

who
is the red-eyed troll
under the bridge
who waves to us
pass over pass over

Behind the Kitchen Door

is where the Devil beats his wife
when sunshine strikes through rain.
Rosa said so. I sat twisting
pigtails she'd plaited, listening

to stories of a daughter my age.
She called her my twin
while I doodled with grits she served
from the black stove. Anytime

a beam flashed on wet windowpanes,
I hopped from stool to kitchen door
to catch Satan in mid-blow,
sure that Rosa would protect me.

Six states and years away
I held a crying baby girl
and listened to my mother keen
across the miles. Rosa's girl,

she said, dead. My darker sister,
shot in Rosa's yard,
flung like a doll on the front stoop,
Rosa rushing out,

the young man yelling, *See what I done
to your baby?* In court,
when sentenced, he turned, swore
to come back and do the same

to Rosa. To Rosa, Rosa
who knew what waits
behind a door, knew what falls
is not always rain.

Straightening Pictures

My parents askew, the whole
hall washed in a grainy past. Mother jumps
in black and white from a diving board, her slim
ankles crossed, right arm flung

high as she holds her nose. Opposite, Father holds
a cocktail shaker and smiles, planked boards
of a beach cottage behind, sand beneath his dark
loafers. The only color—Mother

tinted at sixteen, spirals of red
hair, face creamy as a Madonna. Slanted
to the left—the lone shot
of them together. On a dock, spangled

water everywhere, they wear summer—
Father's easy white sleeves
rolled, Mother in bolero halter and long stripes. Anxious
to set them straight, I see this couple as happy hour

descends, a house-party that sinks
my father. In these frames of a world young
as Eden and without me, the two of them stand
side by side, beautiful and light-stricken, before

my mother lost her footing, slipped
to her sickbed, while downstairs Father kept
company with a glass and the TV, dim reflection
of ballplayers and bewilderment in his eyes.

Storytime

Sometimes I miss the parents of my early
poems, dramatic mother and tragic
father or perhaps the other way around,
tracking their downhill journey as truly
as memory and love allow. Once

upon a time, bedtime tales were my father's
alligator yarns, gentle Ollie
who lived in our attic, loved Cracker Jacks
and Coca-Colas. Ollie, who never put anything
scary in his glass like the tumbler that crashed

one night near my place on the floor,
an amber stain on my open book. Mother
scooped me up—adored doll snatched from her
fairy tales—and rocketed us out the door
of a bachelor friend's apartment, leaving

my father and the man shouting at each other.
In the parking lot, she bashed the side
of their friend's car before we roared
through Columbia's uptown streets, clipping
a Chevy along the way. After we got home,

Mother locked the front door, turned to me.
Let's read The Wizard of Oz *tonight, darling.*
Up the stairs we went. Nothing
had happened. Nothing at all, I told myself,
and sealed that habit into my circuits ever after.

The Magic Bed

after Stanley Kunitz

At times we're under the Sistine's
looming finger or beside the Graces that flowed
from Botticelli onto the folds of Mother's sheets.
Her high, spooled mahogany I climbed aboard,
nightgown tucked and pigtails
flying as we sailed the pages of her books
beyond that brick bungalow on Enoree.
Worlds opened like Fabergé eggs. *Abracadabra!*
Glistening on the banks of the Neva,
the Hermitage danced Mother's ruined legs

and my bare feet through amber halls to city squares
where we breathed air steamed from the bronze
nostrils of horses. Like Alice we tumbled, small
to large, to El Greco's bodies, ghostly,
deliciously chilling. The Nile streamed us to pyramids,
rivers of sand, a dusting from those gods of sky
and earth. *Fee fi foe fum*—the dreaded Tower groaned
with cells of iron bracelets and slits exposing scaffolds
on the Green. Colors bled through pages. Hesse spilled

from books stacked on eyelet linens. When Milton spoke
of blindness, Mother recited. When she was gloomy,
Voilà, we pulled the fabrics of Matisse around
our shoulders and set off for Paris. She steered our fearless
ship to inescapable, separate destinations. When, finally,
I steer her wheelchair down the halls of the National Gallery,
we greet Goya's rosy-cheeked Duke like a long-awaited
companion. Looking up, she says, *He winked.*
Did *she?* No doubt she did, and did and did.

The Kiss of Water

after The Last Supper

Wanting a freer tempera, Leonardo mixed
oil, varnish, and pigment when he tainted
the dry plaster of that refectory wall.
Five hundred years later, Milanese rain slashes
Santa Maria delle Grazie church and the line
outside the monastery, while all eye

the door for revelations of the restorer, her eye-
sight failing after decades of fixing
history. She follows a timeline
of centuries of over-staining,
scrapings, chemical splashes,
bombings and other assaults. Walled

in, she inches along a wall
that began to weep before da Vinci's own eyes
watched dampness ooze from the brick, wash
then flake his fragile texture,
plaster betraying the painter
before, an old man, he left for France. Mold signs

Christ and his disciples, faces outlined
in triangles that embrace the refectory's fallen
moment portrayed in the painting;
just after Jesus speaks of betrayal, of lies
to come, he looks beyond the plates, knives, the matrix
of pewter and glass on a table forever awash

in twilight. Glazing the room, a gloss
from three windows in the work blurs the confines
of the hall into a landscape lost in a mixture
of blues and browns. Disciples stir from the pall,

stricken. Crooked fingers curve inward—*Lord, is it I?*
Forming his own triangle with pained

arms outstretched, Christ reaches down the painting.
One open palm offers bread; the other, on the harsh
tablecloth, reaches for wine. Jesus is the eye,
the disciples, rope lines
pulling away and toward him. Out of the wall's
powder, Judas, Peter and John, a fixture

of paint's recovery and ruin. The broken lines
of Judas's hands as the left washes over the bag of silver,
the right mixes shadows with spilled salt. His eyes buried in the wall.

After Andy,

Andy, Andy, his Jackies, Marilyns, comics
    and green stamps, the animals saved

        from extinction by slashes
            of red, blue, yellow—the zebra a rainbow

of lines—after ghostly screens, print
    and film—a world of mirrors, everyone drawn

        through smoke out of all that he unmasked. Coded
            versions of the Last Supper, his last work—

an alchemy of Eucharist and secular, stenciled
    and hand-painted—Christ with Dove soap,

        a rosy bird hovering, three disciples circled
            by GE's blue logo. Death stamps the work

unfinished, left in Elvis's shadow, in shades
    of hibiscus unbound by stem or vase, a garden

        floating on curves of color. Freed from
            wither or ruin, petals and heads disembodied,

the blossoms move beyond any frame
    and anyone who reaches to touch.

Between Worlds

for Margie

Her arms flutter, as if
      to flee her body, the milk

glass hands skimming sheets
        like autumn wings:

thumb and fingers open and close,
      perhaps to pluck a word,

sometimes pointing to say
        a name or spread

into a trembling fan as lungs surge
      inside her chest, the way

that burst of sparrow, trapped
      on my sun porch, charged

the frantic air, beating,
      beating against God's hard light.

Red Wolf to Coyote

In truth, I am not
you, wearer of phantom fur,
shadow of myself.

My brother, gray wolf,
would have you, cousin, for lunch.
If lonely, I may

open my den for
a coupling. Close kin. Too close
for me and the man

who sees you when I
cross his field. You run over
the land; my blood runs

from time and mankind.
Man plots his own path and place
on earth. He forgets

earth turns for the night's
moonflower and for each owl
dropping hair and bone.

The Man Who Loves Broken Things

They speak to me from curbs, dumpsters,
wherever they are left. Each split table,
ragged broom, armchair spilling stuffing between its legs
like a Thanksgiving turkey makes me grateful.
I dream of shears oiled, sharp again, the lamp lit.
The boys laughed all those years in Daddy's store,
the way I couldn't leave damaged goods alone.

Before papers slap wet grass, my old station wagon
is winding the streets, slipping behind malls,
back with the cardboard and the Styrofoam.
I wait for dark to unload. The bathtub fills
with rakes, coat racks, umbrellas and rolled-up rugs.
Two hoses and a porcelain basin
behind the sofa, the sideboard's stuffed

with blankets, a birdcage under the bed.
After the neighbors sent the city men
to peep through the windows and poke around
the yard, I moved what I could off the porches,
filled Mama's Buick and pulled the doors to the garage.
Shut it up the way I did her bedroom
after they took her off. Now Mama's bed is full again,

toasters, trays, wheel rims raising the patched quilts.
Magazines and newspapers line the sun room,
right up to the ceiling, so those people across the driveway
can't see inside and come after the TVs and tires.
I *know*, just the way I know that little kid
down on the corner picked up those chains, dragging
them home. I chased the boy, yelling,
I want my chains. I need my chains.

The Woman Who Loves Takeout

Ring the bell and leave it,
I tell the little green grocer
who runs orders.
Money's under the mat.
Saves me from stores where I hide
behind cereal boxes, likely to park
the basket between the coffee

and cokes, then bolt.
Couldn't stay at my job after they brought in
computers, copiers. And the commute—trucks,
vans bearing down. I walked away, left
my car in the lot, keys and all.
At home, I vacuum, pressing down

the way my iron flattens a wrinkle.
No calendars, clocks chopping up the days,
time turned into obligations.
Just listen to that phone—
ringing with *oughts*
from everyone: my ex, my son,

the doctor who prescribes the pills I save.
Though nothing else piles up, everything
on the porch waiting for Goodwill.
What a mess
we've made, the world
sinking under our accumulation.

Melancholia

Grandmother's word, Churchill's black dog, gift
from his father. Who can know the way that gift

sifts through the blood, silent as snow, fluttering down
like a great-aunt's tablecloth. Who can say why the gifted

close the door, that child so good,
so quiet. Or the uncle cheerful, bearing gifts,

who drives his long black car alone, says his wife
is fine, just fine. The caring brother of lost gifts,

phones to speak of low black clouds, dog days—
barely a drizzle, but coming down. Where is the sun, giver

and taker that follows its own path, dark and light
the same to those who go alone. Where is the son, a gift

from the gods, whose black phone
rings and rings. You give yourself the gift

of time. *It may rain. It may not.* The shift
comes when you enter the dark fog's drift,

feel the mist, damp and closing down—know
only this: *It may lift. It may not.*

Goddamnitalltohell

Katherine Anne said, in a gravelly voice. *Cat*, everyone called
her, friend of my mother, mother of my friend
who told me those were her mother's favorite words. Cat said them
when she called long distance and the operator answered *sir*, said them
when she stood in line to vote and was denied, because records
showed—deceased. *Goddamnitalltohell, that's my husband.*

*I'm his Goddamned widow and I'm here to cast my Goddamned
ballot.* She threw Bloody Mary parties after church,
and when we opened the front door and the dachshund slipped
out, she said those words, shouting, *Shut the Goddamned
door before Jimmy Dean gets caught in the street sweeper
again.* Jimmy Dean, with knotty rivulets braiding his shiny back

and a corkscrew tail, zigzagged across the yard. Our parents drank
Cat's bloodies, tall glasses black with cracked peppercorns, swirling
with lemons, vodka and a little tomato juice, while we played jacks
on the screened porch or rolled marbles down the sandy drive. If we
kicked volley balls into her exquisite garden—*Goddamnitalltohell,
keep those Goddamned balls out of my iris and the Goddamned roses.*

Few understood the roller coaster that took Cat from high
anger to the deepest wells. No meds then, only *Goddamnitalltohell.*
But she didn't curse when she drove children to the Veterans Home
to visit, and to pick mushrooms under the old oak. And all
she could do was weep when I called to tell her
my mother was dying. After clearing the sparse apartment, I took

Mother's crystal bowl to Cat as no words could thank her enough.
I stood on the front porch, breathing in the fragrance
of jasmine, remembering the last time I heard her say those favorite
words and Mother said, *Hush, Cat. Hush, and eat your salad,* that
shrimp and avocado lunch Cat had brought, along with narcissus bulbs
she would kneel and plant beside my mother's back door.

Music

    for David

Tonight, we walk
    down to listen
        to frogs. Shrill,

insistent, their song
    surges from the black
        pond. Around

our feet the grass
    creeps, transformed
        by tiny black

creatures, those first
    wet crawlers
        to leave

water. A tidal
    wave of drumming
        rises for the most

slender of moons.
    This two-note
        chorus beats

a single heart
    and doesn't give
        a rat's ass

about sadness.
    For this brief
        time, neither do I.

Pawnee to Wolf

I.

Did you see
        our shadows in firelight, dancing
in your fur, black wolf,
        under the moon? See how we
crawled to buffalo, your head
        on ours. See us
on our knees, when Medicine Man
        worked his magic.
White wolf of the north,
        when sky covers sun and ground
with one cloud,
        will you lead our hunters
through earth's white halls to the chains
        of caribou, rabbit and mouse?
Without you, the people
        will have only roots, berries
and the blue wind's wail.

II.

Do you know a tribesman walks
        four times around his house
when he causes your death?
        Your sacred flesh is left
for coyote, fox, magpie and raven,
        who calls to all
and is also holy. Do you know
        we sell your pelt to the crazy Tannik?
When the white man set out
        the poisoned meat, you lay

on the prairie choking
    as did ferret, eagle and fox. Grass
became poison
    for pony, antelope, for the children
of their children.
    Our fathers wept.

III.

Look down Red Star, Wolf
    of the eastern sky. Look down,
Fools the Wolves Star,
    trick your brothers into howling
before Morning Star burns.
    Spirit Talker,
when the conversation of death
    has ended, be my guide,
your voice higher and higher
    until you and I
sing no more. Until you are
    the breath
that moves the clouds to open.

Letter to Sallie in Mallorca

You must be painting the almond trees
below the purple mountain, groves twisting upon groves
beyond your terrace. Sad news from our old
town. Now Talley with lung cancer, so soon after
his sister's—forever in her wake—such closeness.
Is Ira able to come to Spain again?
Is he worse? Our daughters far away—where
is Augusta aiming her camera now? Elizabeth

sold an oil of the marsh. Her gallery struggles—she struggles.
Francis sends cheers and requests another dance
with long, tall Sal. We can see you—all angles in black—coiled
and ready to unwind in that beat-up pavilion over the creek.
Your Chevy stuck in reeds and pluff mud. Your crazy driving,
our laughing with Peg—she got us going until we screamed
Faster! What a threesome we were—laughing, crying, egging
each other on. Thanks for the old photo you sent. Look at us

vamping it up, hair shadowing our faces, dark lips dripping cigs
as the record spun "Smoke Gets in Your Eyes." Paint the blossoms,
Sallie, spill them over canvas after canvas while sheep
across the road, with backs gray as the stones
of your house, rise on hind legs to nibble the half-open
buds, their split hooves crushing the ground's flowers. Once
you said, *I'm not lonely as long as the light lasts.*
Paint them now. Paint it all, before the sky turns.

Songlines

> *For the animal shall not be measured by man...they are other nations, caught with ourselves in the net of life and time...*
> —Henry Beston, The Outermost House

In Alaska, searching for the wolf by day
and longing by dark for his howl,
I spot a body, gray fur sunk into bone
beside the rails as the train speeds deeper
into Denali, a wilderness where
all things move with the seasons. The pink
of fireweed dies to floating cotton

as August lengthens. *Canis lupus*—
science named him—will plow snow to tear
the white weasel and hare, nuzzle
young in the camouflage of a den. And over
summer's green-gold tundra, trail
caribou, mile after tangled mile, plunging
streams that redden and twist with salmon.

This mythic, hunted animal—the Pawnee's
Spirit Talker, the west's *Lobo*—listens
for raven to call from a sky
not yet stolen. When the same sky
streaks with twilight, somewhere
voices rise to it and to each other,
a wild harmony haunting the unknown.

The Beast and The Innocent

Of course, dogs and cats go to heaven,
my mother announced from her deathbed.
Welcomed into heaven, my childhood cat
will groom Grandmother's canary, feathers the same
yellow as the black cat's eyes, the bird

he ate when I was seven. In paradise
pointers lap at duck ponds while cockatiels
screech and perch on each dog's white- or black-
spotted back. Heaven's way is,

as we have heard, *the lion lying down
with the lamb.* A place where Christians kindle
the eight candles of Hanukkah, Muslims unfurl
prayer rugs for Hindi, and the roped Tibetan prayer

flags flutter good fortune for the Chinese.
The wine and wafer bless a round wooden table, a feast
celebrated with unleavened and leavened,
mango and oyster, babel unlimited. And the spaniel
that killed my brother's rabbits will lie

on the wide-bladed grass of my youth, all manner
of four- and two-legged creatures leaping
over him, some stroking the red-and-white silk
of his fur for pure pleasure, for the grace.

My Brother Sings

after Raymond Carver's "What the Doctor Said"

He sings *when the dogwoods are blooming* as I drive
him and his wife along the highway from Asheville,
away from a hospital where we waited in the doctor's office,
sitting in gray chairs, joking about my allergy

to their six cats, how I can't sleep in their house
and still breathe. I watched my brother move
his fingers over swollen knuckles that he used to
crack when I was little just to tease. There to hear

the results of the lung biopsy, now we know.
Traveling through Blue Ridge mountains, we see
dogwoods, redbuds, cherry trees heavy
with April's abundance. When my brother

begins the song, his wife in the back seat on her cell
interrupts, *Dabney, will you please stop singing
while I'm telling Sis you have cancer? Oh, sorry,* he says.
He glances at me while petals drift with us

down the mountain. Our laughter's almost soundless.

Winged Wolf

after Taryn Rubin's "Edifice"

You see him, cicada-like wings lifting his form
from an artist's collage. Beside you now, aloft

and featherless, he glides
to an oak's branch. The handsome head tilts

as crows caw and flap from trees. Floating over
crisp lawns, the gray-and-white body is transported

by shimmers of filament, a chimerical hovercraft
with fur and legs swaying above the red bicycle

in the drive. Like a hummingbird at the trumpet vine,
he dips into hemlocks and the green

of dogwoods. Tonight's dream will ferry him for miles,
luminous, high above traps, gunshots, dynamited dens

and one sheep chained and trembling bait at someone's fence.
As dawn claims him under a scoop of moon, you will watch

this soaring creature, not Pegasus or Icarus
branded by the sun, not held to the earth, but Canis

Major of the night, fabled glow in the pantheon of stars.

After the Hands

work the earth
    to row
        its seasons

free the clay
    the paint
        the pen

to write
    the voice
        to tell

the story
    that makes
        the music

what can
    the body do
        but sing

Author's Note

The work of others, whether it is visual or written, is always transporting. To enter their world is my goal, and some of these poems are the results of those efforts. It's for the reader to decide whether I have brought them along with me.

I regard the wolf as the ultimate other. Wolves speak to me from beauty, strangeness and vulnerability, representing both the beast and the innocent. Their voice is the music of the wilderness. I am eternally in debt to Barry Lopez for his masterful book, *Of Wolves and Men.* In that book, he cast a brilliant light on the world of wolves and the tragic effect of men on that world. Lopez calls the wolf both substance and shadow. Also, the more recently written *The Secret World of Red Wolves,* by T. Delene Beeland, is a fine account of the valiant efforts in the Carolinas to reintroduce the red wolf into the wild and save that species from extinction.

As for the beasts and the innocents these poems speak of, this writer feels there are many that are sometimes two-sided—like the god, Janus—and hopes that they will be discovered by the eye and the ear of the reader.

In the poem *"Raised by Wolves,"* the phrase *all that vulgar beauty* is from Elizabeth Bishop's poem, "Roosters."

A close friend once said that I have a lot of people inside me. Maybe that is what has drawn me to persona poems. For a number of years this form has continued to be a challenge and a delight to me. Add to that the stories I have heard from my own family. They stay with me and will forever be a part of me —as is the voice and presence of my mother, who showed me the way to beauty, to art, and how it may be what saves us.

Acknowledgments

My gratitude to the editors of the following publications, both in print and online, in which these poems originally appeared, some in earlier versions and differently titled.

Arroyo Review: "A Senator Celebrates"
Atlanta Review: "An Artist Speaks to her Unborn Paintings,"
  "My Brother Sings," "Goddamnitalltohell"
Broad River Review 2014 Contest Finalist: "Yeats Exhibit, Downstairs
  National Library, Dublin"
Cave Wall: "Melancholia," "Rosabelle's House"
Conotationpress.com: "After Andy," "This"
EKPHRASIS: "The Kiss of Water"
FutureCycle 2012: "The Magic Bed"
Green Mountains Review: "Fallen Gardens"
Iodine: "After the Hands," "Straightening Pictures"
Kakalak 2006: "A Spinster Considers Her Options"
Kalliope: "American Tourist, Normandy"
Main Street Rag: "The Man Who Loves Broken Things,"
  "The Woman Who Loves Takeout"
Nebo: "Behind the Kitchen Door"
NineMile.org: "Pawnee to Wolf," "Winged Wolf"
Pedestalmagazine.com: "An Artist Speaks to her Unborn Paintings,"
  "The Dance"
Persimmontree.com 2011 Contest: "*Raised by Wolves*"
Persimmontree.com 2014 Contest: "Letter to Sallie in Mallorca,"
  "The Bridge Game"
Redheadedstepchild.com: "Music"
Still Point Arts Quarterly: "Soir Bleu, 1914"
Streetlight.com: "Between Worlds"
Thin Air: "Gray Wolf to Dog"
Wild Goose Poetry Review: "Songlines"

"An Artist Speaks to her Unborn Paintings" was the 2012 *Atlanta Review* International Poetry Award winner, and "The Kiss of Water" won the 2010 *EKPHRASIS* Award.

The following poems were included in *Alchemy,* a chapbook published by Main Street Rag Publishers (2004): "Elizabeth Plays Alice," "Behind the Kitchen Door," and *"La Maddalena."*

Anthologized poems are as follows: "The Beast and The Innocent," *Imagining Heaven* (Central Piedmont Community College Campus Printing, 2010); "The Coal Bin," *American Society: What Poets See* (FutureCycle Press, 2012); "The Beast and The Innocent," *...and love...* (Jacar Press, 2012); "An Artist Speaks to her Unborn Paintings," *What Matters* (Jacar Press, 2013).

Many thanks to Allison Elrod for her invaluable contributions to this collection and to Leslie Rindoks for her perceptive reading of an early version of the manuscript.

The beasts, the innocents and I have been blessed by the eagle eye and editorial skills of Diane Kistner, and it has been a fine journey.

I'm extremely fortunate and deeply grateful to be guided by friends and fellow poets, Louise Barden, Eleanor Brawley, Barbara Conrad, Mary Crews, Maureen Ryan Griffin, Mary Kratt, Rebecca McClanahan, Ione O'Hara, Gail Peck, Barbara Presnell, Dede Wilson, Terri Wolfe, Lisa Zerkle and Irene Blair Honeycutt. Special thanks to Irene, who created a home for the literary arts where the door continues to be open to us all.

Cover photo, "Two rhea feet among the hands," by Gillian Montgomery and Leah Holoiday (goneforwords.com); author photo by Gay Pender; cover and interior book design by Diane Kistner; Bodoni text and titling

About FutureCycle Press

FutureCycle Press is dedicated to publishing lasting English-language poetry books, chapbooks, and anthologies in both print-on-demand and ebook formats. Founded in 2007 by long-time independent editor/publishers and partners Diane Kistner and Robert S. King, the press incorporated as a nonprofit in 2012. A number of our editors are distinguished poets and writers in their own right, and we have been actively involved in the small press movement going back to the early seventies.

The FutureCycle Poetry Book Prize and honorarium is awarded annually for the best full-length volume of poetry we publish in a calendar year. Introduced in 2013, our Good Works projects are anthologies devoted to issues of universal significance, with all proceeds donated to a related worthy cause. Our Selected Poems series highlights contemporary poets with a substantial body of work to their credit; with this series we strive to resurrect work that has had limited distribution and is now out of print.

We are dedicated to giving all of the authors we publish the care their work deserves, making our catalog of titles the most diverse and distinguished it can be, and paying forward any earnings to fund more great books.

We've learned a few things about independent publishing over the years. We've also evolved a unique, resilient publishing model that allows us mainly to focus on vetting and preserving for posterity the most books of exceptional quality without becoming overwhelmed with bookkeeping and mailing, fundraising activities, or taxing editorial and production "bubbles." To find out more about what we are doing, come see us at www.futurecycle.org.

The FutureCycle Poetry Book Prize

All full-length volumes of poetry published by FutureCycle Press in a given calendar year are considered for the annual FutureCycle Poetry Book Prize. This allows us to consider each submission on its own merits, outside of the context of a contest. Too, the judges see the finished book, which will have benefitted from the beautiful book design and strong editorial gloss we are famous for.

The book ranked the best in judging is announced as the prize-winner in the subsequent year. There is no fixed monetary award; instead, the winning poet receives an honorarium of 20% of the total net royalties from all poetry books and chapbooks the press sold online in the year the winning book was published. The winner is also accorded the honor of being on the panel of judges for the next year's competition; all judges receive copies of all contending books to keep for their personal library.

www.ingramcontent.com/pod-product-compliance
Lightning Source LLC
LaVergne TN
LVHW020939090426
835512LV00020B/3433